Trekking from the U.S. to the Caribbean and Canada—wind at their back, ear to the ground, listening for "the logos of what trembles underfoot"— the poems in Music For Exile glean an inheritance of lyrical, received and invented forms to beckon a "mythic assemblage," an aggregation of personal and historical losses, intimate and en masse. In poems of place, poems of encounter, domestic epics and epistolary calls, deGannes locates exiled music in the caesurae of one immigrant woman's arc and troubles the ache, that "ironic hunger for home" when home is itself a vortex of violence. The poems trace, retrace, crossover, "draw poison out" and "fissure desire," enacting and inviting an expansive reckoning of all that has brought us here. They demand the journey be worthy and sing into being a radical sense of belonging. *Music For Exile* is Nehassaiu deGannes' first book-length collection of poems.

✳

"What an incredible accomplishment! Nehassaiu deGannes has deftly and expertly crafted a book of poems that will shake you to your core, remind us from whence we came and shake loose our homesickness and shaky memory. This book made me weep. It is a revelation, as breathtaking and beautiful as Nehassaiu herself. It is a journey through landscapes—both interior and not; it coils and unravels. With an acute eye, and observations so detailed in her recollecting, all the details are like fine lace dusting our wrists on long velvet sleeves, or the tops of feet on long cotton madras skirts. She offers heartbreaking stories of pain and torment; of survival and forgetting, the forgetting necessary for survival and the slow recollection of those seeping through in safety. DeGannes doesn't let you linger and savor nostalgia. She shakes it from you with a brutal story of abuse and/or violence. Then she turns around and soothes with an ocean breeze and the subtle flavor of sweet guinep. I did not want it to end."

—CYNTHIA OLIVER, Choreographer, *Queen of the Virgins: Pageantry and Black Womanhood in the Caribbean*

"It seems we're all traveling/the circumference of a creole skirt,' yes we are when the journey's map is Nehassaiu deGannes' first book, *Music for Exile*. Sail a global Caribbean, where 'home' is Chile, Brazil, Iceland and Jordan. Take a moment on land with folks like Kamau Braithwaite, Harryette Mullen, Jay Wright, Kate Rushin. You ready to 'blossom: sweet corn; raw pine; the plum kitchen cosmos'? Here's your chance, a fresh voice, unafraid of labels or schools, formalism/experimental in the same poem. The same line! A vortex where politics and race, reportage, athletics, history, and etymology all whirl in the gyres of poetry. And love. DeGannes lives in the place where poetry is born— shout hallelujah!"

—BOB HOLMAN, *The UnSpoken, Sing This One Back To Me*

# Music
*for*
# Exile

*

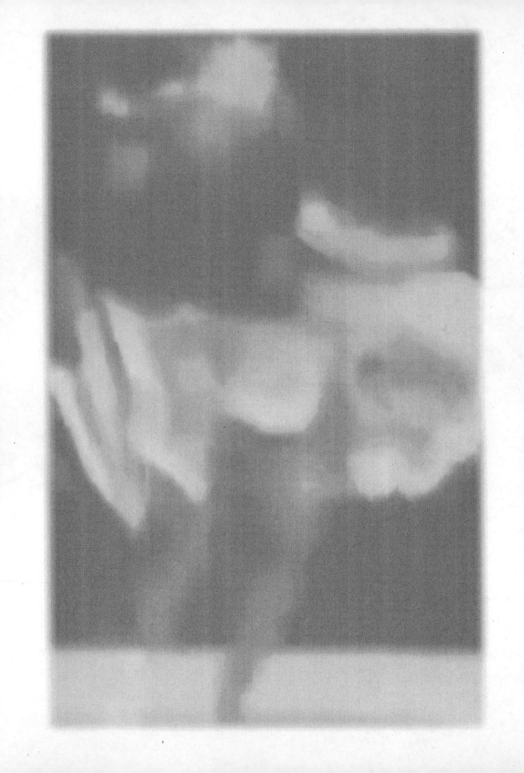

# Music
## *for*
# Exile

## Nehassaiu deGannes

Tupelo Press
North Adams, Massachusetts

Music for Exile.
Copyright © 2021 Nehassaiu deGannes.
All rights reserved.
First edition: February 2021

Library of Congress Control Number: 2020946966.

ISBN: 978-1-946482-46-4

*Designed and composed
in Dante by Dede Cummings.*

TUPELO PRESS
P.O. BOX 1767, NORTH ADAMS, MASSACHUSETTS 01247
(413) 664–9611 / editor@tupelopress.org / www.tupelopress.org

Tupelo Press is an award-winning independent literary press that publishes fine fiction, nonfiction, and poetry in books that are a joy to hold as well as read. Tupelo Press is a registered 501(c)(3) nonprofit organization, and we rely on public support to carry out our mission of publishing extraordinary work that may be outside the realm of the large commercial publishers. Financial donations are welcome and are tax deductible.

This project is supported in part by an award from
the National Endowment for the Arts.

NATIONAL
ENDOWMENT for the ARTS
arts.gov

# Letter for Khadejha

Hummingbird   servant of hybrid Light
and of Asé to the
twelve tribes which are scattered
abroad  Greetings

Caught your exhibit at the AGO this August
Entering the Millennium  Didn't even know
you were there in the room at the end
of the corridor of British painters a few Henry
Moores  Picasso and some African masks

I was reading again   still reading
and writing  Trying to get at
family connections: uprootings
displacement  How is Coquitlam?
Do you like the climate?  Wooden frame
houses?  Looking colonial  Just like New
England   with the addition of mountains?

Imagine?  We've all left
Montréal  Amuna and Nzinga in Toronto
Kamari on the west coast  PhD in Anthro
managing a women's drum ensemble
speaking of which there's a woman
you should meet: Christabel
will drown you in drums

Did you know that summer in Dominica
we roasted breadfruit at the center
of an island?  Pont Cassé  In a hurricane
shell of a house  Roast breadfruit   avocado and fish
A regular *bouzai* Creole band and all  I read
Chistabel played chanting *moon*   calling
*Oya*   already present in the roofless room

I can't say
her drum entered my body and the moon rose
below me and the *bouzai* were stars
but all was a flickering vessel  rocking and
rocking and somebody's palm leaf
kept whispering *this is you girl*
*this is you*  just like Dionne  so I landed
not ready to find myself
home

January  I've arrived
in Providence  Lynch calls me long distance
thinking he's routed me out  Declares me Trinidadian
Did you know deGannes are only found
in Trinidad Grenada and New Orleans?
Seems he knew daddy  Trick
is I already know him  Met his sister by way of
mommy  It was Christmas in Toronto
She's estab. the first school for learning-disabled children
in Port of Spain and tells me all about her brother's book
*Nightmare Overhanging Darkly*  So I buy it
teach from it  And here he is
claiming he's found me  Seems he knows me
from Sonia  Wants me to read at a tribute
I go to Maryland  Read  Sit 1 2 3 tables
away from Haile Gerima *Bush Mama Sankofa*
Have you seen his films?

I didn't know you were from Philly
Which means you were trekking north
*Are you boiling cloth in the mountains?*
*Are you teaching?*
all the time I was trekking south
*Have you erected any totems?*
*Are you hungry for cotton?*
I see you still work with your hands

That afternoon I left Amuna
I walked up YONGE ST. and heard drums
A group of Nyabinge brothers at the corner
of DUNDAS and one sister in a circle
of Eaton Centre shoppers  My feet stood
Waited 45 minutes for a glance to take me there
corporate highrise: shimmering Kaieteur
*have faith girl*
*have faith in the things that bring you here*

No  I wasn't surprised
when I exited China-
town and found you there *Cerebral*
*(All My Relations)*  Your signature floating
damballah style  Altar'd wax resist
textiles  crystal bowls and Orisha bells  An offering
of breadfruit made of newsprint papier maché
I wasn't surprised  I simply registered loss

It's been a long time Girl
A long time  but it seems we're all traveling
the circumference of a creole skirt
Her spinning scatters us so

June  we went to the river
5 women: yahNé Salamishah Onyx
Asali and I  trailed the ark and the dancing
skirts' swirling amber  Stood at the bridge
offered oranges to the Schuylkill
and the priestess in white  looking magnificent
in her wheelchair  raised hands  made a slow
sign of the rainbow  Humming-
bird in South Philly

Would you know me if you saw me?
I've cut my locks but my face
remains the same  I'm trying to do what you do
but in language  Mythic assemblage  Bleed through
Wax resist  These feet are shy  Still I work
to enter  When was the last time
you made it home?

# CONTENTS

✳

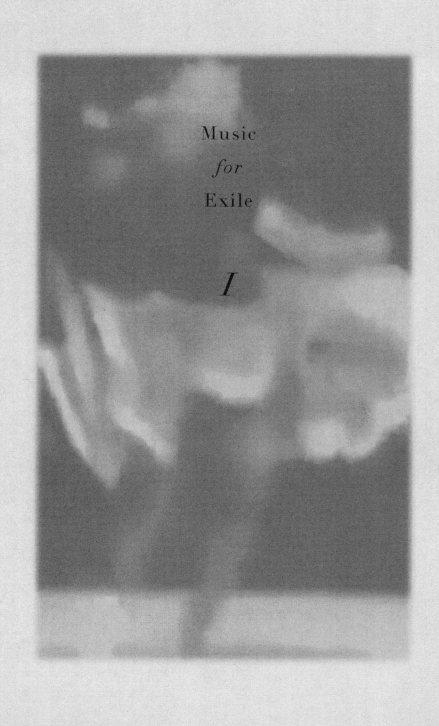

Music

*for*

Exile

*I*

# Mutter

I have lost two children, a hand to marry, some change, a few pair socks.
A gathering of blue hydrangeas. What's left, but a few pair unmatched socks?

I have found some friends, books, available apartments, a discarded rendering
of a bathing nude, dresses I have liked and worn and socks.

My niece S is a tempestuous yogi.
Golden unruly hair and certain hands, she's always wearing Lion socks.

On tabernacle mornings, in the canine hush and rush of trains, I stare
at other women. Pregnant, would I remember to wear socks?

Would I borrow my husband's sweat pants, his faded jeans,
or cusp my waist in a pink sarong, and tuck my hands in socks?

"To have enough for my own Home Team." " To fill a barn."
Secondhand prams, consignment bibs. "How 'bout those Pawsox?"

A light shoe worn by comic actors in ancient Greek and Roman plays.
1) puppets 2) tourniquets 3) Graffiti on the overpass: "SCHOOL SOCKS."

For three days, ice made love to the limbs of trees. It was wondrous.
The terminal shuddered to the grounded man, "LaGuardia's been socked."

In a painting (somewhere): a rocking chair, a shaft of golden light.
A woman sits, immersed, content. She is darning socks.

"My first childhood home?" I have no memory. No basketful of birdies.
No wet yarn on the line? Just the skunk of sulfur like diesel's sour sock.

The refinery's eternal flame, its canine-caramel-sweetness, was our oil-yard Venus.
Yellow flare on a hazy horizon. Night's white tear in God's sock.

J, you are wisdom's brother, our water-boy and drummer—
"He'll be a man one day," I am crying, I am crying for the love of socks.

Today, the sky is freshly laundered. Look, how the garments catch the wind.
Lay it down, Nehassaiu, the wet yarn's trundle, the tug and stretch of socks.

# Undressing The River

Slow, salt-fired

Abandon the beach—
*that oppositional miracle of hot, black sand, the volcano's sputum of sparkling shit—*

to the cruise ship.
Pick your way.

Rewind music to its source.
*What the trees drop*

Mountain kiaso: mango, copra, banana dung
*Your feet could stagger through*

and get caught? Be stuck here forever:
*Two nodes on the island's primordial web.*

Spot her? The cow (tamarind brown). Horns!
*She spots you. Grow very still.*

It is said:
Columbus' men from their vantage lost at sea took one look and declared Waitukubuli,
"a crumpled heap of paper,"

clutch a sheaf of land, squish it into one's fist then toss it on a sea-faring table.
Et voilá: the impasse: "Dominica."

Leave the riverbank to her: the logos of what trembles underfoot.

*not the gutted estates, not the airport tarmac stocked for export, not the wait for IMF
and EU subsidies*

Step back into the river.
Back onto the rocks—some jagged as the day the volcano dropped 'em

And walk

# One Fine Philadelphia Morning

In a mansion on Walnut
our black heroine awakes.

Our black heroine awakes.
Knowing she's alone, sleeps more.

Knowing she's alone, ignores
the antique doorbell ringing

in a mansion on Walnut.

The antique doorbell ringing,
the downstairs phone's eruptions,

the downstairs phone's disruptions
do not disturb our heroine.

Our heroine is not perturbed.
Friendless in this new city—

The antique doorbell ceases.

Friendless in this new city—
The staircase sighs.  A door creaks.

The staircase sighs.  A door creaks.
Arthritic trick of the wind;

just the wind's arthritic tricks?
Our heroine sighs "hello."

Friendless in this new city—

Our heroine rises, "Hello?"
Peers down the railing's cascade.

Peering down the dark cascade:
sees the thief.  She's not alone!

Does the man see her?  She's stone!
His back to her, he tiptoes.

Our heroine stifles "Help"
    ✳

His back to her, he tiptoes,
down, down with a small black case.

Down, down with a small black case.
Dispatcher picks up.  Whisper.

Dispatcher picks up.  Whisper.
"Ma'am, speak up.  I can't hear you."

"Ma'am, speak up.  I can't hear you.
Is the suspect a black male?"

His back to her, she tiptoes.
    ✳

"Is the suspect a black male?"
dispatches old souls dusting,

old black souls dusting the rails—
of her grad school studio.

In her grad school studio:
DuBois and Ellison march.

"Is the suspect a black male?"

DuBois and Ellison watch:
The phone.  A cop's loaded gun.

A cop's loaded gun.  Her phone…
"Yes, he's black."  Her tears are black.

"Yes, he's black."  Her tears are black.
Aren't all our heroine's brothers?

DuBois's and Ellison's march.

# Fugitive Witness

set down your wheeled box
set things right

bells on your ankles
bells at your wrists

adjust stray tassels
dust epaulets

select top hat
stroke the coal-black felt

tap your temple
unmoor your hands

stir the cavern
with gold-tipped wand

commence to pulling
as if smoke as if stars

on a lengthening flag
all those lynched notes

swelling
your heart's piano roll

all those blackbirds
pouring

# "Yes, He's Black"

The air in my closet is black.
Black are the shoes I am sitting on.

My mother and father are black.
I am a black violin.

No bluebirds wiring ahead?
"I am not dead."

*Dance me through the panic 'til*
*I'm gathered safely in*

I'm quoting Cohen
in this coal-black city of 'trane?

I'm quoting Cohen
in this city of Coltrane.

The television's gone, the stereo's
gone from the downstairs parlor.

The talk-radio's gone—
That all-day quarreler.

And what was it
He was carrying so delicately?

*Prodigal servant with a breakfast tray*
I the stalwart widow; He the hearse

This whole old house quiet as a dead-end.
4 squad cars. 8 police officers. 8 guns at the ready.

No bluebirds wiring ahead?
*Dance me to your beauty when the witnesses have gone*

If in the aftermath, the staircase stutters?
"An antique clarinet with gold keys."

# Night, A Suburb

Night.  A suburb, U.S.A. Afro-Sappho's
newly adopted son arrives.  His mother,
only 14, had hidden his coming in-
to the world. She was

a big girl, even before waters gathered
'neath the pockets of her grey XL hoodie,
even before an internet chat room and
the screen name she'd been

willing to meet.  Flesh?  What bid her rise and go
from her safari desk? "Hyena?" "Lion?"
Soft willing somnambulant queen.  "I like you."
"Think you're beautiful."

Man-hole of simple words.  Entranced wildebeest?
Where exactly had they thought to meet?  Well, Clem
is here, crooned lap to lap in Sappho's living room,
pockets the round sleep—

He's the animal we've been awakened for.
Born of the wild surf.  A rustling at the back
of the sea's trundling throat—Oh, Oh, Oh-Oh-Oh?
Tides.  Tidal pull.  Thirst.

The strangeness of arms rocking out to raise Clem,
does not open nor even flutter his eyes.
*The gods' carnevale: the taking on of flesh.*
He's content to trust

in the benevolence of all water.  What
clamors is not the careening need to "say
something:" like "Only" like "Punishment" like "Seed."
The knock meant for me?

Huddled on the high wooden verandah— eyes
drunk: "wildebeest?" "lion?" "hyena?" "giraffe?"
Memory's slope congregates the water's edge.
Guiding us from bed:

Hosts? Kikuyu calls rapping at the suburbs
of a dream? Just the mystery of waking,
arms raised. *Come.* Look. Clem's open mouth is a bell.
This house is a church.

And, just as suddenly rain recedes. Goes where?
An adolescent mother slips back to the
forest of her life. We animals glisten.
Prey and predator—

drawn, gaunt hollows shimmering, fold front shadows
to the ground and drink. What labored truce names us
mother, father, sister, brother? What famine?
What uncommon thirst?

# Album

Gently weigh.  Now trouble the blue
door, embossed with the outline of an island.

Parents are an island. Dark suit.
Pillbox hat.  Square, simple veil.

No other family fills the frame.

Imagine love's small galaxy:
dashiki'd comrades—glasses lifted,
a giggle of champagne.

Lift the vellum veil. Hush.
Put a finger to my mother's dress.
Embossed satin.  Creamy hourglass.
Note my father's steady gaze.

# The Poet Dreams of Her Father

stooped under the stairs, dark monk at his scroll,
painting my new pine desk. Things his hands make

blossom: sweet corn; raw pine; the plum kitchen cosmos
of heart-leafed Wandering Jews, Dad liberated

from four plant-less pots, abandoned by the last home-
owner. With Benedictine patience, he watered—

waited for what slept in the dirt's silent fist.
Mornings, I watch and wait: stubborn; a daughter.

Will another whorl of blossoms soon appear?
Faint bruises on my mother's arms and wrists.

I demand a fuchsia desk. Exacting (like Lear)
a child's ransom for my father's household kingdom:

"Not pink enough." "Not pink enough!" Vexed.
He stoops lower, mixes paints, brow furrowed, perplexed.

# Sonnet & Stumble

A vortex invades the house.  In the sump
of sound decelerated, I wait for
years to erupt.  Then, in pink pj's, I soar—
super-hero (or small *soucouyant*) to triumph.

It is night.  Moleskin.  Molasses.  Cavernous night.
Father creeps upstairs.  Mother's on cruise-
control to the couch, sashaying wine.  Bruised
lip: lost wasp on the edge of her glass. She rises—

"Imagine this?" Her fingers pirouette
the delicate stem, then circle the living
room  air, "We vowed." "We heard Robeson singing."—
Her sea-legs, lonely, as a stranded . . . Rockette's.

In the heavens above us, a toilet flushes.
My brother's sleep salvages on.

# Home Movie: Gretel As *La Femme Nikita*

Yesterday, my brother and his friend, Jim,
took a black marker and scrawled fierce mandalas
between my bed and mirror.  Mandela
survived twenty-seven years in prison,

but can I survive my father's logic
that *I* have until tomorrow to wash
*their* decalcomania off my walls?
I'm stoic, even pedagogic.

Scrub really hard, but their graffiti isn't fazed.
Morning revolts: we are all getting ready
for school and for work. Dad stands, steadies
his hand, belt twitching like a lava trail—

I've grown old.  Shift my book-bag from one cramped
shoulder to the next. Catch my mother's eye:
Is fear life's grand design? He beats her: I step in.
He beats me: _____ Well, the canonical lamp

blew up—flooded the crash-scene of my heart.
And that's what set me to running

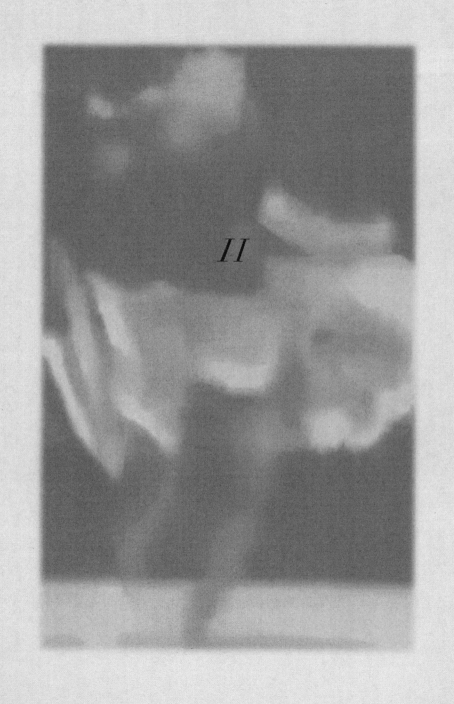

*II*

*It is music for exile... for the symptoms of migration.  It is the languishing music of picking through your belongings and deciding what to take.*
—Guillermo Verdecchia

\*

# Boston Bridge Works, 1927

On our left we have Narragansett Station
    See how red dominates the horizon?
        Brick  Lights  Sky

Consider the three  upright   substantial
      our Moses  Nicholas  John  Notice at dusk
          only the far one blinks (first) a warning

for birds or the dead  Slip off your shoes  Feel
      yourself rotting  wood  exhausted iron, *oh that*
          *saxophone sound*  Well it's not worth repeating

but wind takes up residence
      with power  You know gates latching  unlatching
          shiver of light on rain soaked wire.

Folks whisper it's steam riding these towers.  Me
      I've been walking this tour since 1763  The year Mary
          Wamsley slipped a white-picket child into boiling water

Believe her blood lines the sky?  I know what's not
      Escaped  Free  & her own children too.  Not *negro-*
          *mancy*   Girl worked that case in high court

See for yourself  Step out one morning
      with just enough light  Red wanes
          Axe ceases & Mary's sweeping back concrete

broom like a cenotaph (semaphore you'd say)
      whisking saltwater  warning arrivals *keep moving*
          No future at POINT ST. LANDING.

Wonder what that is?  Well the meaning's as clear as
        clear as gold in a BENEFIT window  Funny how
                sun's a ventriloquist   tricks you into hearing

*life* where there isn't any
        Now that wall's like my friend
                Has a house in Riverside

From her deck you can see
        one catalpa tree clear out to crippling water
                (FRONT ST.'s downriver, hotels and all

Still she can't fathom her neighbors:
        whole lot grown wild   heads with wings
                barring acquaintance with

hurricane swells
        Wonder did Columbus make of this place?
                This is India Point   *softly now*

hindsight blesses land *Tri-ni-dad*
        Land  See there   Our own POWER ST. Trinity
                Now what brings you to Providence?

Tracking one family's greed.
        Pardon, you're tracing your family tree?
                so sorry  Wind's got my ear

# Ocean Voyager

"Sepia Swan"
        mother quivers
                at my cheek
"let this face
        be your passport—
                smooth as cream."

I float
        out of port
                New Amsterdam,

legs snuffed
        under water-
                silk skirts.

I Tubman
        other Creole
                daughters across.

Mount
        the distance, fixing
                my one good eye: how

precisely to balance
        the crimson (serviette
                & egg-white (gloves

nesting at her fugitive
        knees; Sally
                is about to be

engaged.  Sam (her Yank
        does his best
                not to look at me.

"yeah
          though I walk
                    through the valley"

Late,
          so very late,
                    it's early morning . . .

old moon
          chortling my cigar's
                    stubbed star— unlaced

cambric
          & fluttering
                    eye-let,

corset
          & pantaloons—
                    I give myself

wholly
          to the horizon.
                    Penumbra legs

on the ship's
          rail: "I'm free."
                    Tomorrow,

my glass eye—
          open as
                    sunlit water

shot
          through
                    a telescope, I'll meet

Sam's eye;
        Refusing
                to look down.

Water-silk.
        Damascus steel.
                Foulard mandarin collar.

Refusing
        to be the one
                explored.

# A Catch of Shy Feet

*Five Golden Shovels for Mary Wamsley*

I

A catch of sky: slow-dusk tobacco leaves flagging the wind
like a field of zigzag turkeys, tangled,
trussed. Unable to fly.  Among

kettle screams, pots clanging like bells—
I wring n' chop. Backwards from fourteen. Then fourteen again.  There.

Safe in the 'Not-Yet" of indentured birds of this world: 'Free' is

promised sugar on a mother's lips. 'To Free' is the spiritual
task.  Chubby arms tug at my apron.  New laughter?


II

*To*
hoist him up to my hip? Steady his blue gaze with mine? Refuse
his baby-groping for my scarf, the knife, the
fire? To quiet the live racket.

*To*
clean his face of jam.  To unbutton my breast to his mouth. To mutter
the names of my girls into his oatmeal hair? No.
*Down*. Down to
the sea to The
Floor. *Up?* Oh little bird, I am caught in the master's net.

III

Hands cracked.  Blade bright!
Still.  Alone in my lameness
to split freedom from

the bone of hard work. *How many years*, shy feet? My
eyes have scoured this kitchen; shirking the beautiful
blade's dis-ease.


IV

What stays me like Abraham?  The sacrifice at
last must be clean to the heart, to the
sparkling house, to the gods of this boy and the father-root

cause of all frightening unflappable things.  Oh, Bird-burdened hip, what of
mine? All gone to the neighbor's stock. What of us? The
kettle? The pot? The gap—the welcome steam of its blackness? Will

I unhinge his warp, his little harp of a
body from mine? I will buckle my heart's wild

*Down. Down.* Little crown. Little feet.  To bird your sweet inflammable
soul 'to the 'whirling-place.' *Down* to the whole whistling lung, I must stuff.

V

I am fugitive, then pulse, then wind—
All my daughters' hands tangled
in mine.  Saturate in sky among
the dizzy trees. We are free!  My skirt bells.
Oh, little flag surrendered to the water, There
will always be that knocking. An opening when a Door is
a boy is a boat. Yes, Courthouse, I carrion.  I Charon. I spiritual
exodus. Always my heart catches with his laughter.

*We hear from Hartford in Connecticut, that one Day last Week, the Mate of*
*a Vessel lately arrived there from the Coast of Africa, being delirious, took a*
*Negro boy into his Arms, and jump'd into the River, and drowned himself*
*and the Boy.*

# Amulet

outstretched hands
as if above the head is life
head. seed. bell. a note
resound a click redeem a clack. a quote
intoning sighs what life is after

elbowed ascension. water
dis winged crick de whispered crack
lose shekere. loose shackle
the dark wood rattles

the dark wood rattles
*Mermaid. God's Gift. Success. Friendship*
what salt? *what's left?*
trade limbs embrace him. snare

so descend. bird in mind. no bush
waves reassembling flight
turquoise gold. still life

# Ironweed

*In 1734 . . . Angèlique, a Black slave of François Poulin of Montréal,*
*was told that she was to be sold. In her fear and resentment she set fire to her*
*master's house. The house and other nearby property were destroyed, and*
*Angèlique was arrested convicted of arson and sentenced to hang. A rope was*
*tied around her neck, signs bearing the word 'Incendiary' were fastened on*
*her back and chest, and she was driven through the streets in a scavenger's*
*cart. Worse was to come: she was tortured until she confessed her crime before*
*a priest; then her hand was cut off and she was hanged in public.*
 —Daniel G. Hill, *The Freedom Seekers—Blacks in Early Canada*

Heavy black boots crunch up HOPE
ST.  So this is Providence, Rhode Island.
My tongue is dubious of New England names:
BENEVOLENT and ANGELL appear and reappear
in thick circles of air.  Across LLOYD, I run
purple woolen fingers along a strophe of iron

bars, tasting dates hammered into iron
plates.  Here, history gives itself away.  MOUNT HOPE
is not a mountain, a fort, not even a church, but a day-care center run
by women.  Mothers who come from the islands (not this island),
leave on mornings.  Now at dusk, they reappear
purple silhouettes against a chain-link fence, whistling names.

One child quivers at the hiss and ring of her name.
In the Antilles, a wet finger kissing hot iron
flickers the way a snake's tongue flickers — a woman reappears,
then disappears, begging light at my grandmother's door.  She hopes
to reclaim a body; she has come for her island
daughter.  A tropical silhouette, I run,

wading thick snow until I can't out run
the years anymore; even streets shed their names.
HOPE belts EAST looping south to BLACKSTONE — *la ceinture d'isle.*
So I bury the belt to my traveling dress under the iron-
weed next to a paling fence, a sway-backed serpent molting hope
of everlasting life.  Saltwater souls appear to disappear

from this New England town.  Once, in New France, I appeared
a cardboard plaque for a face; black ink running
incendiary language, a mother's reverent hope
for a daughter—HELLO, MY NAME IS: MY FATHER'S NAME
IS: IN CASE OF FIRE, CALL—Now my feet really feel like iron
*belle* bruised and weighted, ringing this plantation island.

An electric crucifix crests that real mountain island,
where mother and child are sighted.  Reappearing.
At dusk, white lights twinkling on a skeleton of iron,
we begin our thunderous descent.  Blood runs.  A river runs
down my brown thighs.  Yes, menarche shares its name
with moon: this flowering fist is a vain stump of hope.

I sigh ANGELL; *Angèlique* appears.  In a flickering red run
a siren's angelus, Rhode Island ignites the palingenesis of a name.
My bilingual retina hosts her smoldering, my ironic hunger for home.

# Lost Planet

It is music for exile . . . for symptoms of migra . . .
tion.  It is the languishing. Pick
through your belongings.  Decide what to take.

My face? That photo? Granny's recipe for *braf*? Black cake?
Greencard (tick.) The heart's a camera. Click.
Picture 'an ancient muse of exile.' Name her "Harriet" for symptoms of migra—

Shun the cornfields, the free town ashore the Great Lake
with two black families, first bike, plenty friends? Now stick
to what belongs. Decide what to fake.

Too black? Not black enough? Shake
the definition tree.  Move south. Guard exhibits at the Frick
& join the pan-African suitcase museum of exiles. For symptoms of migra'

(an ocean's tendency to wander back in time) dull aches,
forgetful flags, joyous bursts of heroic
rhetoric for a music that doesn't exist—enter the 125th St. symphony of migra-
tory selves.  Dear Brethren, The Future Might Be Long, so decide what to take.

# When Last—
### *after Kamau Brathwaite*

*(i)*

here I am reduced
        to a mutter of ash
        a harrow of bone
        a dream of meningitis

where I cannot hum home
I cannot shell peas
I cannot quarantine money

my ambition was a thistle in my crown
a vague map   a vaulted ceiling
bright fruit in my pocket   we blanketed seas

I bundled up my wife & my children
"my authority was foot-stamp upon the ground"
I nailed green stars to our palms

here I am reduced
        to a siege of forgiveness
        a flag in my widow's eye
        before the shelter of coma
        the triumphant corn

        in the quiet
        in the absence
        I transform

*(ii)*

    here I am
        a churning sail
        without trunk-mast
        without dug-out boat
        a muttering sheet
        steering a cot

        no plantain
        no fufu
        in my mortar's gap

    here I am
        a sea-wall slap
        a wailing slip at my window
        you daughter-in-law
        you granddaughter
        my grandson
        you bury my son
        in a Canada plot
        cremate him like a Hindi djin
        you creosote
        you nutmeg dung
        I cough you back
        don't stand in my yard
        under my guinnep tree
        don't flood my door
        clinging to me
        don't conjure his face in my porch-lamp's skirt
        I cough you back

*(iii)*

here I am leaping
      precipice wail of banana leaves
      whole mountains cut on the bias
      cutlass waves & coco debris
      I run home

here I am bracketing
      breadfruit & guinnep gossip
      & porch-lamp blare
      to stand in galvanize prayer
      in a hail of Mami Mary's mourning

here I am pell-mell
      in a hurricane curse
      her black purse brandished
      to bruise bone
      peel rind
      disown my father's face from mine

here I am
      a ginger lily awaiting a gap in the iron

          a bent stalk

          a loneliness
          a loneliness
          a loneliness

          father gone
          grandmother has shut her door

# Refuge

Dear disappeared town, the flowers
at my window remind someone of you. Say
"petunias." Hear *Betunia*—town of his father's birth.
Mornings, my man leaps from my bed to brew mint-
cardamom tea. Hear *sea*. Dear *B*, his father's
found a way to grow fig-trees in Newark, NJ.
In winter, you are safe, burlap-cocooned,
a smuggled-secret in his garage.
No hungry warblers. No sudden frosts.
Nor the Atlantic weight that can slow.

Nor the Atlantic weight that slows
an eighty-year old Palestinian man walking
through Manhattan in search of olive oil.
He scours bright shelves of the city. *Home*
is a map salvaged purely from memory
and the beveled light in his hands.
*Olive oil as smoke. Olive oil as wine.*
*Olive oil as desert mosque. Which orchard.*
*Which school. Which mother. Which son.*
Dear son, come summer, he will lift.

Dear sun, come summer, he will lift
the trees and place them under your ardor,
darning that lost farm with this cramped
garden, for there's only one celestial arbor
we all live under. He will become master-
seamstress, desert bee, oh, pollinating one.
For here lies his secret to the ripening of figs
in Newark, NJ: Prick each fig, every one,
with a needle, dipped in olive-oil.
A man crows, brings me tea and smoke.

My man crows, brings me tea and smoke-
purple fruit from the chain-link garden.
I graze each coppery plum. Say "home."
Hear *Chile, Brazil, Iceland* and *Jordan.*
Seek the invisible navel.  The mouth
is a bulldozer? No, our smoke-velvet lips
warble "witness," join in the map-maker's prayer:
*This orchard. This school. This mother. This son.*
*This fig.  This room.* No one can say gone is gone.
Not the disappeared town, not the flowers.

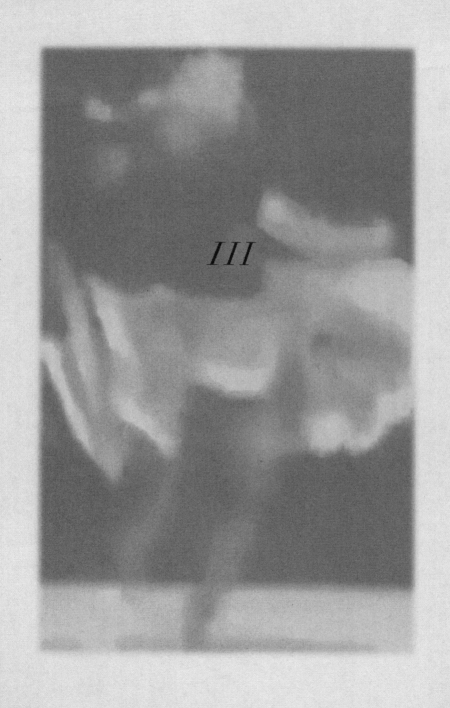

*III*

*. . . she is a pomegranate
pecked clean by birds to entirely
become a part of their flying*
                        —Li-Young Lee

# Isis & Black Madonna
# On X-Roads, N-Roads,
# & The State of The Union "Address"

recall when
all beyond this was page
every movement outside the body: liturgy
every sign ingested:
mass

a movement suggesting blackness: mass
against a cloud as if in sea foam
a coffin tossed   not quite crow
not yet eagle   somehow
a lung breathes in
                            W

now wing

crossed vowels
spoke which way Wind was blowing: scent
is lexicon   scan
left scan right: track sweat:
track blood: track
excrement

crack twigs &
bundle fire into faggots &
name the index finger: stick
stick mud: stick mulch: stick clay
ponder the slick necessity of death
how each hole comes fitted with
wind-chafed seed

X & Y &
Zed:   glossolalia
dangling from a tree is
*corpus delecti*   another kind
of sign: the doubled wing   Word
Word   wood's captive metaphysic

so it is
every movement inside the body: insect
any moment outside the body:
suspect   so it is when
one world ingests another: amnestic sand
always swallows the
sticky finger

# FINGOL: A Caribbean Libretto

*Overture*

Jalousies up
Jalousies curtsy askew
Pink bougainvillea leap into view

Picture a sun
Picture a sea
Figure a wind at hurricane season

❋❋❋

Gretel's parents had to take a trip
Far up north

Had to get on a plane and fly
Away

So, Gretel went to stay
With her Granny, Catherine

Who lived in a house
At 9 Turkey Lane

Jalousies winked
Jalousies clapped

9 Turkey Lane
In Roseau, Dominica

There was grandpa
Aunties and uncles

Hugs and kisses
And plantain chips

There were hellos—my she's grown
What you feeding her smiles

We'll send for her soon

Don't cry
Goodbye

Mommy and Daddy flew
Far up north

Gretel couldn't see them anymore
Even when she squinted her eyes

What she could see was
The man who lived next door
Mr. G

He was not a very old man
Not a very sweet man
But no one told Gretel the truth

About Mr. G
Not even me
Gretel liked two things

To suck her thumb
Play with her bellybutton
Stand at the window and sing

Mr. G  Mr. G look I have my chicken bone
*One day I'll be flying home*
*Look-nuh see all the world was made for me*

Jalousies fluttered
Jalousies flicked
One slow fan batted an eye

At slats appearing
To shudder n' stutter
*Open sesame!* Then,

One day Mr. G
Invited Gretel over for tea
Granny let her go

Gretel was only three
And Mrs. G was never home
For tea and hidden biscuits

Gretel oh Gretel
Where could they be?
Mr. G would task her

My biscuits?
My bonbons?
My sly diabetic's basket?

Under the chesterfield's vinyl pool?
Atop my lemon-oiled walnut
Staircase open chest of drawers?

In the lap of a sleepy phonograph?
Hump-a-bump  Hump-a-bump
Horsey goes over a hill

What's that I spy under your skirt?
What currant?  What button?  What plum?
My raison d'être!  My raisin of ether

And he'd breathe her
Nibble her biscuit
Instead of sweet tea
He'd feed her his tongue

Gretel was three
Didn't like the cud of his tongue
Nor the wet-fowl of his hands

She told Granny No and scolded her skirt
Next time he invited for tea
*He fingoled me.*

*He fingoled me.*
She told her grandmother plainly
So plainly the woman forgot

Everyone forgot.
Aunties forgot.
Uncles forgot.

Her parents up north never knew.
Her grandfather was at work on sweet afternoons
What was a neighbor to do?

Everyone forgot even me
And agreed to more tea
At nine more tea at fourteen

More tea each time
The plane brought Gretel south over-seas

Jalousies blinked
Jalousies yawned
Jalousies slept in this fish-gut rose-water town

Picture a now
Picture a then
Figure a poem unraveling at the hem

When, when, when

Twenty-seven years later
At a kitchen table
In a country far up north

Granny Catherine plucks from her basket
The lost planet
Of Gretel's own pomegranate word

One girl-child's forensic dialect
Demeter's redemptive hunt-and-peck
FINGOL

Six stuttering moths in a lamp-lit mouth
An elliptical orbiting sound: singed wings, bruised rind
Black thread spooled six times round my finger

One drunk constellation

*I wasn't dreaming*
*I really did go to hell*

# Reinvention of a Garden
*after Jay Wright*

Could I invent the drum?
I have made stone  shell  bone
the unopened water

Crabs
Flesh exploding into dream

Loneliness does not glitter
it does not invite the desert

                but comes matter-of-factly
                making a cleft-lip sound   bugs  bits
                finger the window of blood intrepid flowers

                skin desire: thick dancing
                wave-rising vertebrae   throat
                full with glittering insects

                dream sandpiper
                dream a robin running through
                her devitalized shrub

and touch?
more than sand
can contain: vertebrae
driven into gardens   where  (sniff
seconds crest
refusing to close around lines

                lips bathed
                stomach warmed
                my sun-beaten floor

and fissure desire (( drum
through a water-creating wall
bird  bird  bird
two or three windows
invent a room

                              look in:  look up:  look out

# Salvage Blues

On the news, my neighbor's trying not to cry.
Holds up prayer against her widow's grief.

cup a lost shoe to your ear
         you may hear a child running

I sank into my closet, like a whale beneath blue jeans.
Hid my fusillade heart, a wail beneath blue jeans.

you could have leaned your head cool against my inside-hand
         & repossessed every story you would have told me

crook a finger to that ear
         it is your own heart knocking

Thief fly away to Birdland!

*not here not yet*
         it is an afternoon whirring on a sun-drunk screen . . . we park

two dead fathers between us
         *the theatre's being gutted*; the shifting weight of twenty men

Bells of St. Gabriel toll for your clemency
But brothers looking like you will be at their mercy.

Unfreight red trebles world and wail your cargo home.
They've put out an APB!

as in drop LAST TUESDAY . . .
         you will hear *Salt 'Mooshuassick'* & an ocean beyond that

We all are startled glass, wobbling
*Thief fly away to Birdland!*

They've put out an APB!
*They've put out an APB*

Somewhere in the city, an estranged black man
melts down gold keys.

# Undressing The River II

We want to spin
our towels about us,

but stand in the damp—
a tintinnabulation of ankle bracelets

shifting, delicately rocking from one hemisphere to the other;
our bikini-clad hips are two red equators.

The sun peeks through banana fronds,
peeks through two copper keyholes of legs and coral pubic bone,

peeks through the green-soaked signature
of an island naming and renaming itself

in the slow, dark ticking
of tamarind pods, "Waitukubuli" "Waitukubuli"—

in the pulsing flash of a cutlass.
Black tail switching side to side.

To be hushed. To be locked in the shutter's
stuttering cough— Are we a catch?

Skin dripping with light. Still.
Sit still for the camera.

Sweet dregs in a drum? Under galvanized awnings
or centuries' shadow of stacked wooden stalls,

Women still sit— Hands deep in the knowledge of how
to beat coarse cotton clean against the ragged rocks,

how to wring provisions from volcanic ash.
Cassava! Dasheen! Edoe! Yam!  We walk.

The cow, now behind us,
occluded by a coconut palm:

her tamarind eyes; her crown of horns—
disappearing in a keyhole of green fire.

# Vortex

AND FOUR HOURS LATER, AFTER OF-
FICER BRUCE UNGER PUMPED THREE
OR FOUR BULLETS INTO THE ERSTWHILE
FOOTBALL STAR AS HE RAN TOWARD
HIM, IT WAS CLEAR THAT SOMETHING
WAS CLOSING ON ROGERS FAST.

*San Jose Mercury News*


this feeling of being hunted persists
even after the hounds are called off
even after your high school's been integrated
even after you rescue your dreams
from the pocket of another man's coat

I WATCHED THIS KID STAND FLATFOOTED
AND THROW A FOOTBALL 60 OR 70 YARDS
SOME CAN THROW  SOME ARE QUICK AS CAN BE
BUT HE HAD IT ALL  IT WAS AMAZING TO SEE


the propensity towards flat-footedness
among African-American males and some females
has been shown to have direct links
to class and religious affiliation
categories once defined as laws of natural selection
flatfooted males and some females
have a tendency to choose low-lying occupations
those not requiring flight
they are content really
to remain in fields
where the absence of an arched pedalia facilitates
stooping or crouching for long hours at a time
it is a position they find most natural
and while resembling the flight ready stance of a cat
this squat is a proven position of prayer
such figures wait in fields of cotton or sugarcane
for the outstretched wings of a god
to swoop forth and carry them home

"negress" is a most logical and etymological
evolution of the term "pas grand arche"
or "nos gros arch" in the mixed tongue
of the Louisianan creole
for it was early discovered by men of great science
that the large backside of Sarah Bartmann
aka The Venus Hottentot   grew in direct proportion
to the flatness of her feet
the body having the genetic capacity to produce
only so many curves and hollows
consumes this economy of arch or "marché d'arche"
in the ample fullness of buttocks and breasts and lips
in the protuberant flare of the nose
there is little curvature left
for that daintiest of ornaments
among European women of the landed class
the foot

hence the negress' inability
to fit comfortably into the haute couture fashions of her time
thus her propensity to settle into positions
where the foot and buttocks are less likely
to be called upon to serve
the interests of the dreamer
they are most happy
when stooped or crouched in a field
of industrial sewing machines

Gerome Rogers however was not one
to sit lightly upon protuberant flares or lack thereof
he was really convinced he could fly

I  GEROME ROGERS  HEREBY WILL MY STYLE
AND SNEAKINESS TO MY CLASSMEN THAT LOOK UP TO ME
TO MY PARENTS' LOVE AND MY TEACHERS' HAPPINESS
I'M GONE  POSSE I CONNECTION I MADE IT

in the interest of seeking connections
we are probing possible links

between "posse" and "pussy"
and a word of an entirely different species "possum"
in the event of the former  our theory
that it is anatomy not class not power
nor sex nor gender that can best explain
the marginalization of the Negro in the aerial age
will indeed be confirmed
already it is known that the black woman's vagina
or "pussy" in the visceral tongue of the North East and West
is considered to be immeasurably larger
than that most ambivalent of ornaments
among European women of the landed and not so landed classes
the cunt
should the missing link be found to be
"possum"
one realizes little advancement of our thesis
save one minor detail
arched-footed European men and some women
pioneers of the landed class
have been known to eat its meat

there is persistence in being the hunted
even after the hounds are called off
even after your high school's been integrated
even after you run catch a ball
and dream of making it on TV

AT MOUNT PLEASANT HIGH SCHOOL
THE COACHES WERE SALIVATING AT THE PROSPECT
OF ROGERS' TALENTS

AT 4:26 AM  TUESDAY MORNING
ROGERS' MOTHER  DOROTHY COZINE
CALLED 911 OPERATORS TO SAY
HER SON HAD A RIFLE
HE WAS ACTING STRANGELY
HE SEEMED TO THINK
SOMETHING OR SOMEONE WAS AFTER HIM

there is persistence in being the hunted
even after your neighborhoods integrate
even after oppossum assimilate
sensorial faculties retain
the genetic handprint of the hunter

AN OVER-STRESSED
AND APPARENTLY PARANOID ROGERS
FORCED THE EVACUATION OF MORE THAN 200 UNITS
AT SAN JOSE'S SKYWAY TERRACE
HE PEPPERED THE SURROUNDING APARTMENTS
WITH MORE THAN 100 ROUNDS
FROM AN ASSAULT RIFLE

there is persistence in being the hunted
even after your neighborhoods integrate
even after the hounds are retrained
ears still prick
at the fall of flatfeet
rising over swampy and mossy terrain

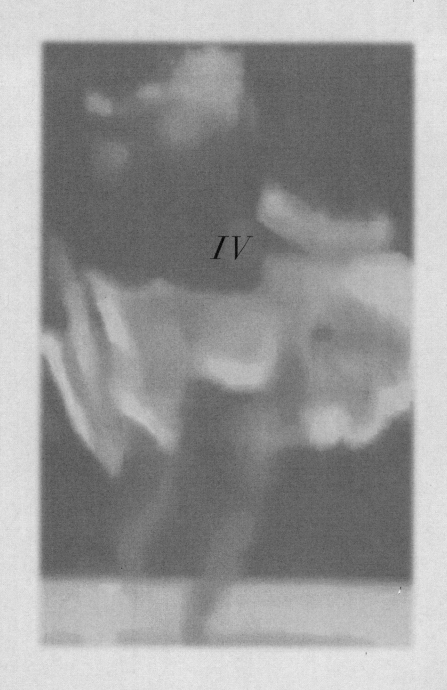

*IV*

*two-headed dreamer*
*of second-sighted vision*
*through the veil*
*she heard her call*
———Harryette Mullen

✳

# Bessie's Hymn

The door, I've been
shouldering

is ajar—a spoon of light, a threshold
of honey—

a cataract, a riot, a trumpet
of honey. To pass through it now is to get wet

with fire or rain, is to be a BAM Hippopotamus woman 880 BC
walking the sunken garden, an Amphora of Honey on Her Head.

The sun's eye winks.  Sterling Brown warbles and Honey oozes, opulently yolks
apiary riches ((( amber dollops ))) into wild black air.

*and all the birds sing bass*

I am paddling up a river of honey

to stand in a field, a child on my hip.
There is no field.  There is no child.  Yes?

I am abuzz.  In this honey-buckwheat field, a child
on both hips.  Honey hands tug at my hair.

MEN I RAN WITH (subtitled) "All the wrong ones."

> One to ©Scrabble
> One to contend in Wolof & French
> One to scratch Adelbergh whiskey from his sand blonde beard.

> An envelope opens.  2 frail petals tumble out. The peony
> in full bloom Monday, washed away in last night's rain.

Even I want to lick the slate clean.  Waggle: "Orpheus
was here.  He came back for me. He held my hand and led"
*and all the birds sing bass*
But now I see.  The Hand
I've been holding all this wild is my own:
a laying on of skirts
petals on the Avatar's crown!
My Banished ones come back inside me to be born
Tuesday through a doorway only honey, honey, honey.

In the dream, Oshun is pulling
Book after Book from my shelf.  They all have my name on them.
"You've been Busy"

She says and the honey spills from her eyes.  She is smiling.
"You are ready."  "You know how to die."

# Isis Prepares for Resurrection

your touch
doesn't feel my flesh
but finds my bracelet instead
a ring of nehesi copper turning my wrist
green like an old woman's arthritic arm
verdant from too much copper

you draw
moonlight towards you
curling sea brass etched with
platinum scars   the eye of the ankh
an anaconda's coil   a chorus
of life and death
I whisper it is just

a bracelet
but your eyes are far
from ornamental   you have
trekked the distance   orbitted earth
and your ears understand
the chained circumference of my upturned palm

this dawn
with both wrists naked
we alone touch a copper band
its pattern like some faint fertility symbol
breath echoing at the source of our hand
we are singing

tenné
to draw poison out
copper to extract a name
I will travel centuries to kiss
your eyes   but cast this arc instead
an alchemical fusion of distance
part covenant   part bone

# Last Surviving Hymn to Hathor

Who leads us, moon-drunk, into clover
and sweeps the starch rectangle of the blank half
of the bed? *You love him? Not?*
Lolling on the dark howl's tambourine.
*Honey, can't find cuz yuh too afraid to die.*
The train is in the cattle yard again,
clattering up and down the lonely tracks.

What makes us cough, plump the pillow, rise
to take a piss, catch the distance lowing in our ears—
Is that Ella all glissando?
What floods our hearts with thunder?
The train is in the cattle yard again, clattering
up and down the lonely tracks.

Look how her tail's a rudder.  Her eyes are bells of iron.
Those daddy-long-leg lashes flint and there are sparks
of hammered iron flying 'bout the room. *Why, when a man
gets too close with a bunch of cow-slip orchids
growing from his fist, you cock your head, go very still—
wonder what he plans on doing with his other fist?*
You're hiding in the cattle yard again.

Pull a ream of paper from the white shelf of sleep
and drown the tinkling cowbells in the toilet's oceanic hiss,
but our conductor drop-kicks her orchestra again
now lounging on your moon-white pillow.
*Fool, love won't find you.  Can't find you.*
Her bassoon now quaking all the orchids in the room.

Why not lay your head down on her chamois lap?
She's scatting an entire confluence for you

of what is done and gone and lost for good
*Life's a dung-hill and you plant your seeds in that*
of what's to come is yours and can be yours to trust
*Not in punishment but in sanctified pleasure.  Cross over.*
*Cross over.* The train is in the cattle yard again.

# Matins

Listen for the tidal thing that tugs at your navel string

The dolphin's somnambular ringing

She began writing and the page illuminated

Her eyes adjusted to the glowing house

Inside everywhere an odd numerological blinking

Outside fog envelops the mansion

One sentry pulsed

The kettle began its slow rumbling

She felt her soul waking up

Will it be enough to enumerate longing?

She'd been coaxing herself to sail round an ending

2 nights ago he shows up at the glass
back door   In drenched hands a heavy brown suitcase 2 wide leather straps
buckled and nothing more

Are they still hurtling towards each other?

She and he

Oneiromantic she is curious

But doesn't let him in

On the machine his voice sounds sweeter than she remembers
It being   but the machine's indifferent ear can't bleed

At some point she fingers the switch because
Lights inside no longer compete with the light
Outside   moon-mist grows aquamarine

A blue cotton-candy underwater forest

She sips tea

Still the problem of an obscene reverie: 2 weeks ago a biking
Accident resulted in his passing   She read the markings clearly
on a yellow flyer in her dream   How it reached her hands
She has no clue

Does he even ride a bike?  & cell phones to confirm

Oh the valley, yes the valley, like a Parsee's tower of silence
on which the past, all of my past, each day is laid to rest:

Her robe slips

The yellow harp is strung

# Undressing The River III

And we walk—
as if from the long horn,
the rattle-gourd, the carnival of memory—
a two-girl crowd jostling the jagged slope.
Towels drunk about our hips like batik skirts
festoon our buttocks, boasting a riotous Hibiscus
trumpeter's chorus: "Come Cousin, let us imitate
the cow's knowing walk." Her *basso*
*profundo* figure eight's. Sly feet liberated from,
but still in homage to, the chained
samba's staggering ship's sway; and
in homage to our Kalinago kin, water-wise,
who knew how to transform, with fire,

tree into boat and rode the salt
off Waitukubuli's volcanic coast
long before Yemaya drowned here
long before Obatala was dragged here
so home extended beyond the black-
ribboned hem of Our Tall Mother's skirt
to include Kalinago villages on Guadelupe,
Martinique, Saint Lucia (now Creole names all?)
Conde's home, Césaire's home, Walcott's home:
"Look, Cousin, we are cousin to this all."

Come. *Leh we brave* Canefield River's uphill course,
its anvil of wince and sting.
Our feet, four stunned
novitiates—toughening, tougher,
getting stronger to find the place
where the Red Rock promises a pool
deep enough and wide enough
to let one's body in.

# At the Red Rock

Here in the shadow of the Red Rock,
recline against your pumice throne.
Graze the cigar bottom and take stock.
Here in the shadow of the Red Rock
all is quiet.  In the next field, the red cock
swaggers.  Far away the airplanes drone.
Here in the shadow of the Red Rock,
recline against your pumice throne.

Become one with the river.
Imagine seamlessness and float.
Sea-drenched gown in a fresh-water mirror,
become one with the river—
Satiate Anchor; salvaged cross, hammered
out of life's blue notes.
Become one with the river.
Imagine seamlessness and float.

Spider the mountain's laughter, "Water—
Blood Trumpet.  Cradled Cup."
Uncoil your dark long locks, Daughter—
spider the fresh mountain laughter, "Caught her."
Become the brass riot of your own French Quarter.
Your Heart: A New Red Hibiscus.
*Oh* Spider, *Oh* Daughter of Mountainous Laughter—
Blood Trumpet. Cradled Cup.

# My Father's Book of Days

Dear P—

You in your quiet city
and me, in mine:

So much has transpired:
I dreamt you one night in Atlantis: white lab coat

*"You're a doctor!"* I swam through the secretive waters.
Must have been the Trumpet vines stuck in your ears.

"Auntie," how 'bout MacFadden & Whitehead?"
S selects the morning soundtrack, cooing…

Your grandchildren await you in sunlit kitchens.
Inside us and inside us, there are several trains.

M, napping, becomes the praying mantis
you'd become in sleep's curious calligraphy:

one knee hiked like a wing or a mountain,
one arm thrown overhead—

each tiny limb, a blood-brush wet with memory.
Fugitive hymns once sung in secret: *Nkosi Sikeleli.*

Stevie Wonder's *Happy Birthday* for MLK.
You were born the same day.

Are you fellow citizens of the *City of Heaven*?
A man stands on the platform squinting,

where the Q crosses paths with the D, blowing
a piped goat's bladder, its keening shadows

my steps.  I am a citizen of this city,
this city, I keep telling my legs.

The lining of the small black case at his feet: red
as vermillion edged pages of old mountain-top bibles

and your black book of psalms.
There are trains. There are several sheets.

Chrysanthemums floating on pine green linen.
This was the summer of repeated motifs. Hafiz writes,

"When the violin is ready to forgive, it starts singing."
And the sheets, the sheets they were cropping up—fierce lyrics

in houses in cities, I would visit by train.
The last sheets you slept on.  The last album you played.

I am singing in this city of poems.  Can you hear me in yours?
"Auntie," she coos, "How 'bout MacFadden & Whitehead?"

# My Brother's Funeral Pallet
# is an Explosion of Flowers

and he burns clean as sandalwood,
and leaves burn green as lizards in the sun.

I wear the white dress he stitched and painted with flowers.

It is late afternoon in Guyana. The light is rugged,
dredged like gold through a day-miner's sieve.

On the road to Timehri, we pass
cassava piled high in cargo-bound pyramids.

I turn to look at my hands.
Evening is a crate the sun enters slowly.

I turn to look at my brother.
Spokes of a wheel chair; slats of a bench—pink-flecked light hunkers down.

The cancerous cells have sent out their call to hunker down.
Two flamingo-pink ice-cream cones beckon from my hands.

"Jump on, jump on," he shouts. "We'll wheel out to sea."
I kick-off n' rudder his tricycle—my pleated blue skirt is the sail.

Two guava-pink cones drip back to my hands.
Leni limps to his wheelchair.

Guava is *terra rosa* mashed to a pulp.
Cool as my hand on his back leading the fever astray.

Some chrysanthemums are red.

Lick the cold-churned cream.  Lick the syrupy paper.
I try to feather it free—

The tarmac is the cracked black back of the lizard we call "Death."
"Granny is lighting the stove to fry fish."

Anthuriums bolt and sail from my hand.
My ears are full of coconut water.

Noon is a halo: a crescendo of gulls. The barrels are studded with birds.
I open the door. Exit the cab. When he is smoke, where will he go?

# Homecoming

White-gloved and perched on the rear hood of the chrome-hubbed convertible gleaming white in the Lake Huron sun, I am one of three girls chosen to be Vestal virgins to the altar of white, Diana's maidens to the Homecoming Queen.   Our white-stocking'd legs and polished white shoes brood statuesque over the rear red leather.   Our white eye-let shivering.   Our white ribbons flagging.   Our white-gloved hands waving and waving and waving to the white faces lining the tree-lined streets lining this small Scottish town.

But the hand inside my glove is brown and the face peeping from the white-ruffled neck of my summer white dress is a beautiful hazelnut brown.   This is my hometown. My legs: two severe batons majorette the hot red leather.   Even after the crowds thin out and the breeze off the lake picks up.   Even after the bagpipes' keen moan fades.   Out past the protestant oaks, out past the immigrants' bell-less church with its small brick frame, its gravel driveway, out towards the cornfields, when only Lake Huron with its lull of tall grasses and only the perennial pines wave back, I am still waving.

# ACKNOWLEDGMENTS

✳

Grateful acknowledgment is made to the publications, in which the following poems have appeared, sometimes in slightly different form:

*Callaloo: The Next Thirty Years* [30:4]: "Undressing The River," "Bessie's Hymn"

*PoemMemoirStory* [Number 8/2008]: "Ocean Voyager," "One Fine Philadelphia Morning"

*Crab Orchard Review (Special Issue: Due North)* [17: 2] "Boston Bridge Works, 1927" *(Reprinted with permission of Providence Athenaeum)*

*Callaloo* [19:3]: "Ironweed," "Vortex," & "Isis Prepares For Resurrection." The latter was also selected for *Callaloo: The Best of Poetry* issue [24:3].

*Caribbean Writer* [vol. 22]: "When Last—," "Undressing The River II"

*Arava Review*: "Refuge," "Homecoming" (Nov/Dec 2011)

*Callaloo* [27:4]: "FINGOL: A Caribbean Libretto"

*After Shocks: The Poetry of Recovery* (Anthology). Tom Lombardo, ed. Sante Lucia Books: "Last Surviving Hymn To Hathor"

*Torch* [Spring/Summer 2010] www.torchpoetry.org: "Undressing The River III"

*Undressing The River*. Center For Book Arts Chapbook (20 pages; limited edition run of 100 copies, designed by Ed Rayher, Swamp Press), selected by Kimiko Hahn & Sharon Dolin:
"Night, A Suburb," "Album," "Matins," "Mutter," "My Brother's Funeral Pallet is an Explosion of Flowers," alongside "Ocean Voyager," "Undressing The River," "When Last—" "One Fine Philadelphia Morning," "Undressing The River II," "Last Surviving Hymn To Hathor," "Undressing The River III," and "Bessie's Hymn."

*Percussion, Salt & Honey*. Providence Athenaeum Chapbook (24 pages; limited-edition run of 400 copies) selected by Michael Harper:
"Letter For Khadejha," "Boston Bridge Works, 1927," "Amulet," "Isis & Black Madonna on X-Roads, N-Roads & The State of The Union Address," "Reinvention Of A Garden," alongside "Ironweed," "Vortex," "Isis Prepares For Resurrection."

# NOTES

*

Each section of *Music For Exile* opens with an epigraph, gratefully quoted from the following:

Kamau Brathwaite's *Middle Passages* (New York: New Directions Books, 1993).

Guillermo Verdecchia's *Fronteras Americanas (American Borders)* (Vancouver, British Columbia: Talon Books, 2002).

Li-Young Lee's *Behind My Eyes: Poems* (New York: W. W. Norton & Co., 2008).

Harryette Mullen's *Muse & Drudge* (Singing Horse Press, 1995), reprinted in *Recyclopedia* (Saint Paul, Minnesota: Graywolf Press, 2006).


As well:

"Ironweed" opens with an excerpt from Daniel G. Hill's *Freedom Seekers: Blacks In Early Canada* (Agincourt, Canada: The Book Society of Canada Ltd, 1981).

"Vortex" contains text found in the *San Jose Mercury News, July 24, 1994.*

Four poems acknowledge the following:

"Letter for Khadejha" samples the *"this is you girl"* refrain in Dionne Brand's *No Language Is Neutra*l (Toronto: Coach House Press, 1990).

"When Last—" borrows its form and one quoted line, "my authority was foot-stamp upon the ground," from one section of Kamau Brathwaite's "When Last Did You See Your Father?" *Trench Town Rock* (Providence, Rhode Island: Lost Roads Press, 1994).

Every word, except for shifts in pronoun, in "Reinvention of a Garden" can be found in Jay Wright's poem "The Invention Of A Garden," first published in *The Homecoming Singer*, now collected in *Transfigurations* (Baton Rouge: Louisiana State University Press, 2000). However, not every word of the original is in the reinvention.

"My Father's Book of Days" acknowledges Alberto Rios' poem "The Cities Inside Us."


Notes on New Forms:

"One Fine Philadelphia Morning" is a variation of a Crown of Sevens, a form invented by Kate Rushin.

"A Catch of Shy Feet" contains five Golden Shovels, a form invented by Terrance Hayes, in which one line from a Gwendolyn Brooks' poem provides the final words for each of the new poem's lines.

*for Sheila, Percival*
*Christopher*
*Catherine & Vaughan*

*for S, J, G & M . . . may your futures be long;*
*may you never be exiled from yourselves*

＊

. . . and in gratitude to the people and organizations who helped hold space for the making of these poems: Rhode Island State Council on The Arts, Vermont Studio Center, Community of Writers, Soul Mountain Retreat, Cave Canem, Bernard & Nicole Georges, Megan Sandberg-Zakian, Phillip B. Williams, Sonia Sanchez, Paul Piehler, Charles Rowell, the late Michael Harper and Aishah Rahman.